FOR THE LOVE OF

HYMNS 2

LDS HYMN ARRANGEMENTS FOR SOLO PIANO

rebecca belliston

FOR THE LOVE OF
HYMNS 2

LDS HYMN ARRANGEMENTS FOR SOLO PIANO

rebecca belliston

For the Beauty of the Earth/Simple Gifts Medley 21

The Iron Rod 12

Jesus Once of Humble Birth/Christ the Lord is Risen Today Medley 17

Master, the Tempest is Raging 26

Moonlight Hie to Kolob 8

Teach Me To Walk in the Light 5

'Tis Sweet To Sing /Jesus of Nazareth, Savior & King Medley 1

TIS SWEET TO SING THE MATCHLESS LOVE

JESUS OF NAZARETH, SAVIOR & KING MEDLEY

Piano Solo

Ebenezer Beesley and Hugh W. Dougall
Arranged by Rebecca Belliston

13
16
mf
19
rit.
a tempo
p
22
25

28
31
34
37
rit.
a tempo
mp
mp
42
mp
cresc.

rit.
a tempo
small notes optional
f
mf
mp
rit.

TEACH ME TO WALK IN THE LIGHT

Piano Solo

Clara W. McMaster
Arranged by Rebecca Belliston

22
27
a tempo
rit.
32
mf
37
42

48
mf
54
59
65
mp
71
rit.
p

MOONLIGHT HIE TO KOLOB

"MOONLIGHT SONATA" & "IF YOU COULD HIE TO KOLOB" MEDLEY

Piano Solo

Ludwig Van Beethoven, English Melody
Arranged by Rebecca Belliston

19
mf
23
27
p
p
32
p
cresc.
37
dim.
espress.
dim.

42
mp
47
51
55
mf
59

63
67
72
77
dim.
81
pp
ppp

THE IRON ROD

Piano Solo

William Clayson
Arranged by Rebecca Belliston

19
rit.
23
a tempo
mf
26
29
f
32

35
38
rit.
a tempo
mf
p
43
mp
48
mf
53

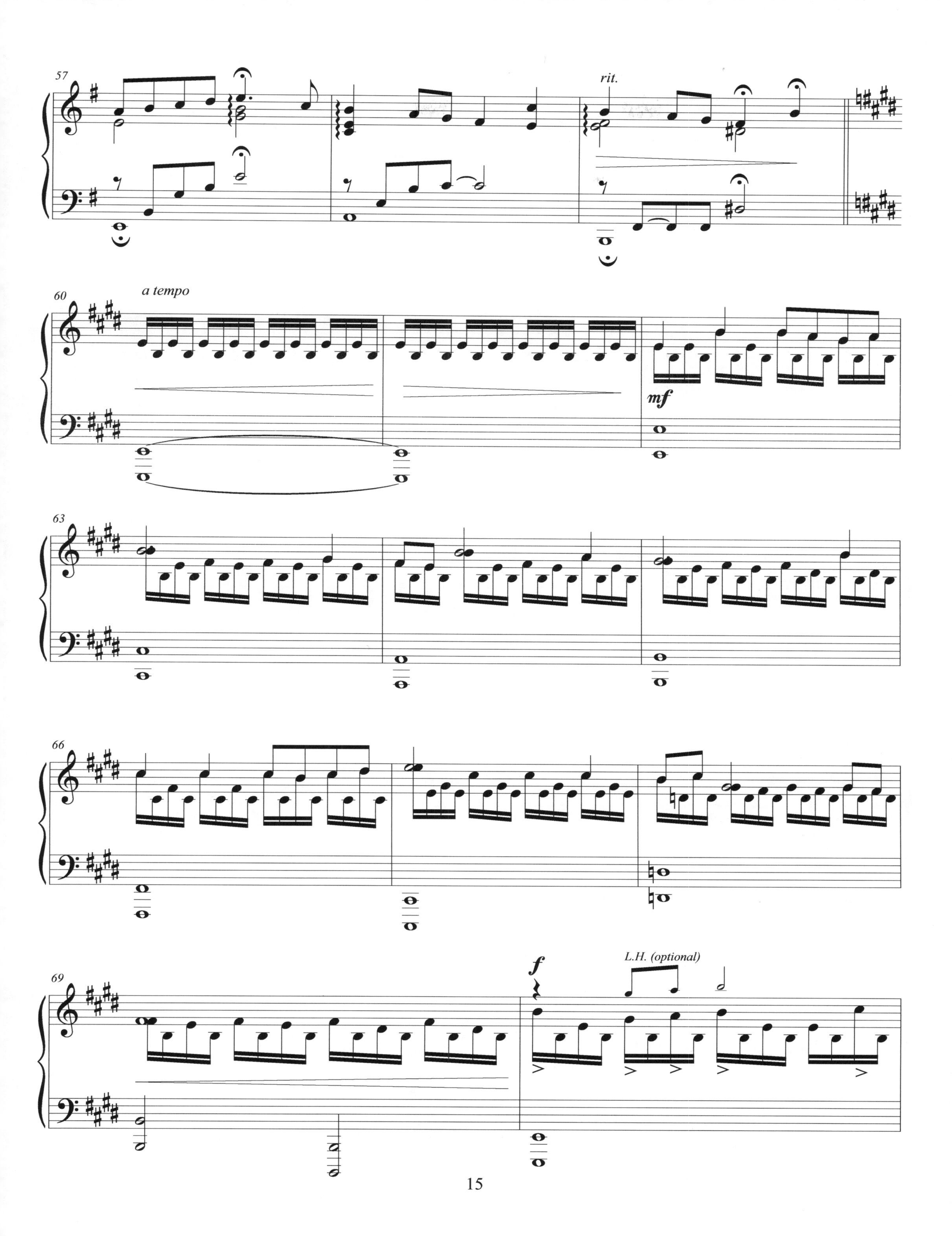
57
rit.
60
a tempo
mf
63
66
69
f
L.H. (optional)

71
73
75
rit.
a tempo
77
rit.
p
80
Slower
mp
rit.

JESUS, ONCE OF HUMBLE BIRTH

CHRIST THE LORD IS RISEN TODAY MEDLEY

Piano Solo

Giacomo Meyerbeer
Arranged by Rebecca Belliston

36
mf
43
49
55
61
68

75
82
mf
88
94
100
f
8vb
106

mp
rit.
8vb

FOR THE BEAUTY OF THE EARTH

SIMPLE GIFTS MEDLEY

Piano Solo

Conrad Kocher & Joseph Brackett
Arranged by Rebecca Belliston

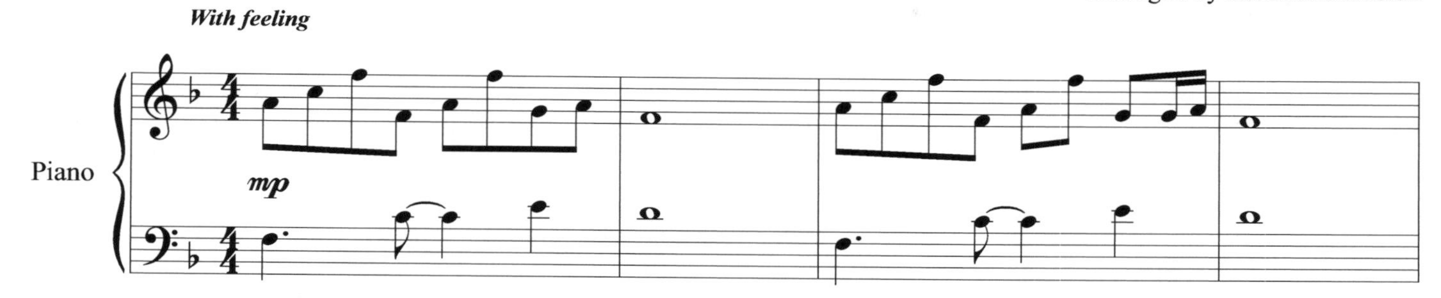

17
mf
21
mf
25
mp
29
33

37
rit.
8va
a tempo
mp
40
(8va)
42
(8va)
44
(8va)
46

rit.
a tempo
f
Small notes optional

rit.
a tempo
60
63
rit.
Expressively
mp
67
72
mf
76
dim.
rit.
p

MASTER, THE TEMPEST IS RAGING

Piano Solo

Music by H. R. Palmer
Arranged by Rebecca Belliston

20
23
26
30
p
35
mp
steady cresc.

38
41
rit.
a tempo
mf
44
47
50
f

53
56
59
mf
63
f
66

69
mf
p
73
a tempo
steady cresc.
77
80
rit.
83
a tempo
p
mp

87
92
96
100
mp
103
rit.
p

ABOUT THE COMPOSER

Rebecca Lund Belliston has been writing songs since she was six, teaching piano since she was sixteen, and has a song stuck in her head at all times. A huge fan of classical, religious, and film music, she composes mostly for piano and vocal. In addition, Rebecca also writes romantic suspense novels. She and her husband have five children and live in the beautiful state of Michigan.

CONNECT :

Website: www.rebeccabelliston.com
Facebook: @rebeccalundbelliston
Instagram: @rebeccabelliston
YouTube: @rebeccabelliston
Spotify: @rebeccabelliston

REBECCA BELLISTON

Original Compositions & Arrangements | Complete listing at rebeccabelliston.com

hymns / religious

- A Poor Wayfaring Man of Grief – PS
- Abide With Me; 'Tis Eventide – PS | SSA | Inst
- Be Still, My Soul – SATB
- Come, and Be With Me/Etude in E – SATB
- Come Unto Jesus* – SATB
- Feast Upon His Word* – SSAA
- For the Beauty of the Earth/Simple Gifts – PS | VD
- For the Love of Hymns – PS Album
- How Great Thou Art – PS | VS | VD | SATB | Inst
- How Firm a Foundation/The Lord is My Shepherd – SATB
- I Believe in Christ – PD | SATB
- I Know That My Redeemer Lives/18th Variation – SATB
- I Will Make Weak Things Strong* – VS
- The Iron Rod – PS | VS
- Jesus, Once of Humble Birth Medley – PS | SATB
- Jesus, the Very Thought of Thee – PS
- Light of My Life* – Songs for a Primary Child
- Master, the Tempest is Raging – EP | PS | VS
- Moonlight Hie to Kolob – PS
- My Country, 'Tis of Thee – PS | SATB
- Nearer Medley – VD
- Nearer, Dear Savior, to Thee – PS | SATB | Inst
- Oil For Your Lamps* – SSA
- Oh, How Lovely Was the Morning – PS | OPD | VS | SATB
- The Sabbath Day* – SATB
- Simply Preludes – OPS
- Souls To Save* – VS
- Still Be My Vision – VD | SSA | SATB
- Teach Me To Walk in the Light – PS
- 'Tis Sweet To Sing Medley – PS | VD
- We Come Unto Thy House* – SATB
- Where Can I Turn For Peace Medley? – VD

christmas

- Breath of Heaven (Mary's Song) – PS
- Christmas Handbells for Children – Handbells
- Come, Thou Long Expected Jesus – SATB | Inst
- For the Love of Christmas – PS Album
- For There's a Savior Born* – SATB
- Hark! The Herald Angels Sing/What Child is This? – PS | VD
- In the First Light – VS
- Noel Christmas Medley – EP | PS | VD | SATB
- Come, O Come Emmanuel – EP | PS |VS
- O Holy Night – SATB| SSA
- Oh, Come, All Ye Faithful – Piano Duet | SATB
- Silent Night – VS | VD | SATB | Inst
- Star of Wonder – EP | PS | Inst
- Where Are You Christmas? – BN

contemporary / popular

- Aladdin: A Whole New World – BN
- At the Piano – PS Album
- Avatar: Bioluminescence of the Night – PS
- Batman Songs: Corynorhinus | Antrozous | Molossus | A Watchful Guardian – PS
- The Blue Planet II – PS
- Cider House Rules/Pure Michigan Theme – PS
- The Da Vinci Code: Chevaliers De Sangreal – PS
- Divergent: Faction Before Blood | Sacrifice – PS | Inst
- Game of Thrones – PS
- The Greatest Showman: A Million Dreams | Rewrite the Stars | This is Me | Tightrope – BN | EP | PS
- Harry Potter: Courtyard Apocalypse | Statues | When Ginny Kissed Harry – EP | PS
- Maleficent: Aurora in Faerieland – PS
- Memories/Canon in D – PS
- Over and Over Again – PS
- Prince of Egypt: When You Believe – PS
- Someone You Loved – PS
- Spider-Man Into the Spider-Verse: Sunflower – EP
- Spirit: Run Free – PS

classical-style

- Andante in A* – PS
- The Betrothal: Processional in E* – PS
- Come, and Be With Me/Etude in E – SATB
- Coronation: Processional in G* – PS
- Dresden: Fugue in F minor* – PD
- The Battlefield: Etude in C# minor* – PS
- Dance: Jig in F* – PS
- The Dungeon: Etude in G minor* – PS
- Etude in C* – PS
- Etude in Eb minor* – PS
- For the Love of Classical* – PS Album
- Fugue in C minor* – PS
- Heart of Red, Blood of Blue* – PS Album
- I Know That My Redeemer Lives/Rhapsody on a Theme of Paganini – SATB
- Jerusalem: Prelude in C minor* – PS
- Leuthar: Prelude in C minor* – PS
- Memories/Canon in D – PS
- Prelude in Bb minor* – PS
- Ryder: Childhood Etude in Db* – PS
- The Sea: Nocturne in D* – PS
- Sonata in A minor* – PS
- Tranquility: Prelude in Db* – PS
- Vengeance: Prelude in B minor* – PS
- The Village: Ballad in E minor* – PS

* Original Songs | P – Piano | V – Vocal | O – Organ | Inst – Instrumental | D – Duet | S – Solo | E – Easy | BN – Big Note